A Pinch Of Yellow

Book of Poems

Krishna Raval

BookLeaf Publishing

India | USA | UK

To my parents,

Punita and Divyang Raval,

whose unwavering love,

constant upliftment, and steadfast support

have shaped me into the person I am today.

CONTENTS

The Quiet

I love the quiet
The green
Sunshine on my back
I enjoy touching the earth
The bark of a tree
I listen
To the birds

Deeper
Into the woods
I find a place quieter
Thoughts still abuzz
Complimenting the bees
I listen
For the rhythm of my heart

Deeper still
I slowly feel
The familiar
A lightness. A dance
Of my subtle body
A steady beat
Calling me

As I inch closer still
I sense the blues
And the yellow
The fun, the mellow
I tune in,
I listen
To the music that is me.

Friend

Dazzling white whiskers and a gleaming black
jacket
A big deal in a tiny, cute packet—
Meet my kitten, my very first pet,
I fondly call her "Mrs. Velvet".

A nimble hunter with a graceful gait
Deep in the shadows she often waits
Sometimes gentle, ferocious at times,
This stealthy cat hides all her crimes.

A whiskered wonder with emerald eyes
Sometimes naughty, and sometimes nice
A cuddly companion on a chilly night
Oh, what a miraculous delight!

She senses when I need her near
Snuggling close and purring clear
I pamper her, she feeds my soul
We keep making each other whole.

Time

Hey, Time,
Let's strike a deal between us—
I will forget those moments
You looked horrendous!

I will try and shut out
Your ugly memories
The havoc you have created
For centuries

I'll not criticize
Or defame you
Nor reveal
That Life's henchman is no one but you

I wish to revel
In this beautiful present
Soak in the elation
I feel this second

Blissfully bask
In this amazing glory
In the magic
Of this charming story

I wish to stay here
Under any pretext
Without worrying
About what's next

Be free from the past
And any future events
The expectations, the anxiety
Or disappointments

For this liberating power
I can con and thieve
Keep them from the truth
Skillfully deceive

Will spread the lie
That you will never hurt, only heal,
I will do this
If you keep your part of the deal—

Either die right now
And don't show me the morrow,
Or rest long
In this moment;
This moment for eternity –
Is all I want to borrow!

Space (A Haiku)

A deep space within
Mirrored by the Universe
I see Her as me.

Illusion

Under the influence
Of this interim illusion
It is as real as it can get
And that if you forget
For a fleeting moment
Of absolute oblivion
You may do things
You will regret
And may not be
Able to make amends
In a series
Of illusory events.

Love

There is a part of you in me
Which I will always see
And you have a part of me
That forever will be

How do you split
The fire from the ash
The light from the flash
It's impossible, really

The fragrance can be gone
The essence, not at all
Love still stands tall
In all its glory

I know it won't come back
Still, I set it free
I'll find peace in time.
In the glorious debris

Disorder and wreckage
Can be a thing of beauty—
It's in the eyes of
The beholder, you see

You don't need someone
With you in person
Or even to know
If they are worthy

You can still have love
That rises above
Distance and time
Or even mortality.

Trapped

All of us are trapped in cages
Carelessly flicking through life's pages
An interesting story, a boring article
Even advice from the sages
A witty ad, a funny limerick,
And of course, those old adages

Little happy, a lot sad
Interested, excited, but also scared
So many moments spent alone
With strangers, many hours shared
In solitude sometimes, and at times lonely
We rarely have our souls bared

Why are we so obsessed
With being extraordinary
Groomed and fashionably dressed
Shunning all that is ordinary
"Pooh, all that is so passé,
And this is oh so legendary!"

"Who holds a higher status—him or them or
me?"
"Didn't wear it better than me; oh, please tell
me, did she?"
"Of course, we have more cars than them
We are almost royalty!"
"The rat race? It's for little people;
Ours is The Grand Prix!"

Do we see the bigger picture?
Do we know our end game?
Do we yearn for something more
Than approval, money, or fame?
Do we know what makes us happy
And what is our true aim?

Take a moment just to be
Stay with yourself; know who is "me"
Be a child, open your eyes
Fan the flames of curiosity
Question everything you hear
And all that you 'clearly' see

Ask yourself what you truly want
What, for you, makes sense
Ask yourself what attracts you so
And what makes you dance
Believe in something, take a stance
Be a person of substance

If you're happy with someone's success
You don't gain from someone's pain
You help the weak and needy
And don't feel disdain
You may still have a chance
Your life is not lived in vain.

Find who you truly are
And that you love a lot
Break the illusory shackles
Which made you lose the plot
Be the best you, a higher You,
You're all that you've got.

Hold Me (A Haiku)

Hold me close today
We will never meet again
Outside our graves.

Heartbreak

I have so much to write
About heartbreaks
I don't know where to begin, and
I don't know if there can be an end.
Isn't it a process?
Like this universe, like nature.

It is like a tsunami
Which washes over you
Desecrating everything
You're made of.
It doesn't stop
Even when the waters recede.

It is like an earthquake
Which disfigures the very foundation
Of your being
And the shocks are only the beginning.
Wave after wave of ruin
Reducing you to bits and pieces.

It is like the iceberg
The tip of which is apparent
But the real havoc is created
By that which you don't see.
A moment of smooth sailing,
And destruction the next.

It is the ghost of a past well-lived,
And loved
It is the twinkle of a child's eye,
Gone with its innocence.
It is the fragrance of a blooming flower
Lost in the storm.

It is also, though,
The mercy of the Creator
The ash of a phoenix
Before it rises again.
It is the darkness before dawn
The winter before spring.

It is the crumbling of the last brick
Before you rebuild yourself
It is like being in a scary tunnel
Just before you see the light.
It is when your knees hit the floor
For respite.

It is the mourning of an old you,
Giving way to someone stronger,
And if you are lucky,
Someone kinder, more loving
Someone more forgiving,
Someone even wiser.

Yes, I have a lot to write about heartbreaks
For each one life put me through
And no, I still don't know when or where
Or how it begins
But I do know, it doesn't end.
It doesn't end anything at all.

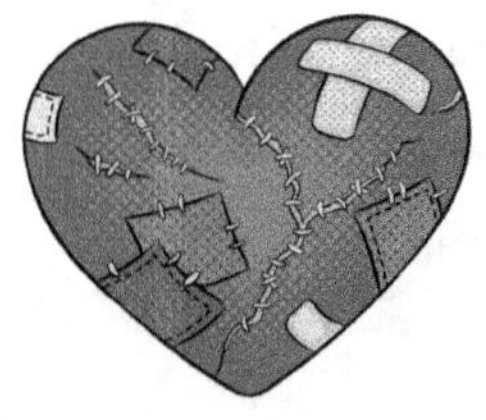

Failure

Stay quiet when you lose
And quieter when you win
Thank the Lord for victories
And when you're in the bin
Be grateful when you're happy
And even when you're hurtin'
When you're on a vacay
And when you're spread too thin

Those who disrespect you
Or mock you when you fail
Are themselves hurt, unhappy,
Miserable and frail
Talking and explaining
May be of little avail
"Deep inhale, and long exhale"
Is my holy grail

Ask the Lord to forgive them
For they know not what they do
They know not what they think or say
Or what poison they spew
Wish them love and happiness
And move away, you do
Not your circus, not your monkeys—
Don't be feeling blue

If you think you're ready for
Yet another fight
I do hope you find and have
Your loved ones by your side
I hope you find your happy morning
After the scary night
Get ready to enjoy another
Roller coaster ride!

Don't Worry (A Haiku)

Don't you worry, love
I will see you once again
When this life is done.

The Monster In Your Head

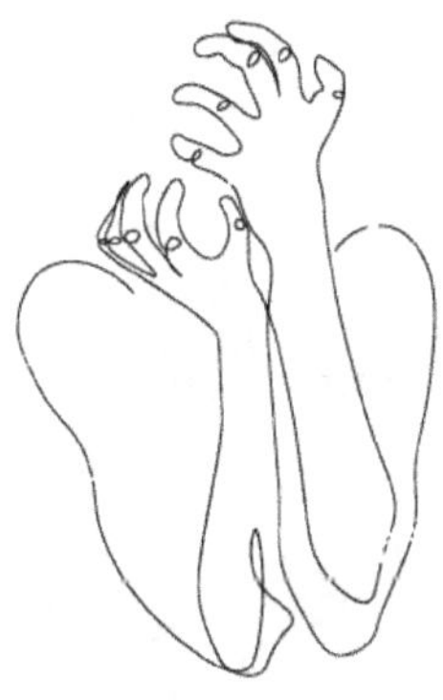

You cannot be defeated
By the monster in your head
Who ties your hands
Behind your back
With an invisible thread
And turns your limbs into lead

No, you cannot let
The monster in your head
Take away all your joy
The will to wake up everyday,
Brush and shower, and
The will to look ahead

Begin to acknowledge
The monster in your head
What it takes away from you
What all it saddles you with
How you can fight it
Or befriend it instead

Oh, you are stronger than
The monster in your head
Cajole him to stay away
To hide, or run,
Or befriend you back
Command him to lightly tread

Grab all your power back
From the monster in your head
Take your life in your own hand
Do not leave things unsaid
Talk with whomever you can
And win over that awful dread.

Today

I haven't felt dread today
Or that I am inadequate
I am not in mourning
There isn't a looming threat
Things don't feel unfair today
I'm not disappointed
I've not been ridiculed
Or bullied
Or felt embarrassed
I woke up not unhappy
I showered and I dressed
I looked ahead towards the day
With surprising zest
I finally feel
I may be enough
If not an asset
I may be okay
For myself, if not the rest
And I am perfectly fine with it
I am not upset or stressed

For whoever, whatever I am
I truly feel so blessed
And hence, today I may be
At my happiest.

Unanswered Questions

Scorching heat, or relentless rain
Where's the rainbow in this profound pain?

Why was the flower plucked before it could
bloom?
Why does the clear sky now loom with clouds
of gloom?

Where is that silver lining people often talk
about?
Is that another thing that must be done
without?

Why are we born if it is inevitable we die?
Why do we laugh when we know we will cry?

How do we hope when we know it can be
shattered?
Miracles? How often are they even scattered?

Where has that spring in the step gone?
Why are those twinkling eyes now
withdrawn?

Why is the river dry, which once happily
flowed?
Why is the face pale which once beautifully
glowed?

Where is that smile which once lit up the
world?
Has it been killed by the stones life hurled?

Where is the melody in that infectious
laughter?
Will that now forever be sought after?

Are there remnants where there was once a
whole?
Remember, there was once a soul?

Does it still speak the truth? Or does it
blatantly lie?
Does it still dare to thrive? Or is it prepared
to die?

Has it been crushed? Or recklessly thrown?
Wounded and grounded and in shreds has it
blown?

Can it awake with a smile in the sun?
Can it laugh again and have all the fun?

Can the eyes sparkle again? Can the glow be
at its best?
Can the heart hope again, or at least be at
rest?

Can the step regain its spring, or even jump
and dance
Can the flower be left to bloom? Is there even
a slightest chance?

Can the silver of the clouds enhance the sky's
blue?
Can the sun shine through rain, and give the
rainbow hue?

Can these miracles happen? Or are these
castles in the sand?
Will life keep dying? Or will death be lived
grand?

One Day

Then, one day
I sprung to my feet
Yearning to dance again
The ones I had been dragging,
Hiding beneath my skirts

Heart beating
To the music of joy
The one I had never imagined
Showing even a glimpse of
On my sleeves

Eyes shining,
Brimming with possibilities
The ones once vacant
Devoid of hope
Downcast before

Then, one day
I finally awakened
From a painful slumber
Where I lived a half-life
With the burden of existence

Yes, one day
I sprung to my feet
Heart beating
Eyes shining
Finally awakened.

When a man..

When a man tells you what you should
Or shouldn't do
It is never just about you
Or your lack of understanding
It is him
Making you feel as less as he feels himself

When a man tells you
Where and how you should improve
It is never just about you
Or your limitations
It is him
Transferring his insecurities onto you

When a man ignores your desires
And touches you without your consent
It is never about you
Or if you deserve it
It is him
Deciding that you don't matter

When a man lays a hand on you
Tells you that you make him angry
It is never about you
Or what you did
It is him
Trying to assert his power over you

When a man deliberately makes you feel
Trapped, hopeless, disgusted, ashamed
It is never about you
Or if one should have to go through it
It is him
Targeting his hatred towards you

When a man says he loves you
And then hurts you, repeatedly
It is never about you
Or whether you deserve respect
It is him
Meeting you
Only as deeply as he can meet himself.

A Muse

He loves you, Life. He adores you plenty.
He is happy and carefree and extraordinary

He enjoys what you give him—pain or
pleasure,
He rushes through time, yet lives in leisure

He values each and every breath,
Unperturbed by the fear of Death

He cherishes and worships you,
Ignoring the damage you're inclined to do

He never lost his innocence
Yet justified your magnificence

He is mischievous, he is strong
He is right, he is wrong

He makes mistakes, he touches lives
He is like sweet honey in your stinging hives

He works hard, has harder fun
He can stand proud and glare at the sun

He stares forever into calm waters
He stands on a hill, soaks in the showers

Man, can he ride for hours together!
Enjoying the wind in the worst of weather

He smiles when you give him reasons to cry
He laughs in your face even when harder you
try

Don't mess with him, Life; he will never let go
Beware! Don't let him hurt your ego

Don't be stubborn, don't be unfair
He'll challenge and confront you and never
despair

Bow down with respect, and accept defeat
He deserves salutations, even Death has
agreed.

Heaven

I once stood at the pearly gates
Of what I thought was heaven
I looked around, what do I find?
There was absolutely no one!

Where are all those righteous souls
Who forever hate 'the gays'?
Who know that we all should love
Only in certain ways!

Where are all those peaceful souls
Who know who all are lost?
Of course, you must kill for God
Because that's what faith costs!

Where are all those pious souls
Who fiercely defend God's honor?
Who stone someone for eating wrong
Or misusing a color?

Where are all those precious souls
Who have beautiful skin
And those who have a certain kind of brain
And those with discipline?

Those are experts on humanity
They know what's right, what's not
Heaven should be filled with them
They make sure who should rot!

Then why is this place so quiet
Where are all the leaders now?
The ones who ran nations, churches,
Temples, mosques, and how?!

I heard someone crying then.
I turned and saw God
This beautiful, majestic Being
Welcomed me with a nod

Before I could ask something
I was zoomed back down to earth
Turns out it was just a dream
Seemed real, for what it's worth

Waking up, I heard a nation
Attacked another one
While I looked around and recognized
God in everyone.

Catch

What did you catch today?
A cold, a cab, or a ball?
Maybe a fish, or a crab,
Or caught up on a call?

Could you catch your train today
Or just a mere glimpse
Caught someone by surprise
Or yourself thinking things?

Could you catch a break today,
Or someone red-handed?
A bus, a flight or any ride
Or were you left there stranded?

A falling star, or a rising one,
A killer or a kiss?
Could you catch a groove today
Was it a hit or a miss?

The predator or the prey
A case, a chill, a disease
Were you caught up in the moment,
Or could you catch some z's?

Did you have to catch your breath?
Or perhaps catch a kite?
A smile, a stray, or a stray smile,
Or someone in a lie?

Could you catch the game?
Or was it a ghost or a grenade?
Was it a vibe, or the view,
Or was it a catch twenty-two?

A mosquito or a movie,
A yacht or a yeti,
A wink, a wave, or a whiff—
Do you catch my drift?

Me

My face is the composition
Of my parents'
My body, the accumulation
Of the planet in arrears

My likes and dislikes
Are so much like my family's
My sense of survival comes
From thousands of ancestors

My values and goals
Come from my elders
And my experiences
Have materialized my triggers and fears

My mind is the cumulation
Of those I've met and loved
I learn new concepts from children
And revise old ones with my peers

The words and phrases
I arbitrarily use
Are the assemblage of
What has fallen on my ears

I know there are parts in me
Of so many other creatures
Numerous places I've been to
And a great many new cultures

I get strength from my friends
Encouragement and solace too
We've shared beautiful moments,
Secrets, laughter, and tears

I still aspire to be more
Inspired by people I know
Poets and teachers
Authors and leaders

And still I have been perceived
As a different version by
Every person who has loved
Or hated me over the years

How can I just be *me*?
If I can even fathom what that is
I am just a bunch of atoms
With many creators.

First Drops (A Haiku)

First drops from the sky
The thirsty earth soaks it up
Oh, the petrichor!

Colored

I've had henna tattoos
A pleasure to be covered in
Even more when colored in
Teased about how much I'm loved
They faded without pain
When I was not looking

I've had tattoos
That seemed permanent
A part of me forever
But they could be erased
Albeit not without agony
But erased nonetheless

And then, there was him.
I didn't even realize
When in places I got cast
With his hue
It was never intended
By anyone

While I was learning
To love the contrast
He decided
We were not the same palette
That we should part ways
And not get stained further

How do I unmerge
Our colors now?
How do I return
To my own tone?
How do I become
Unstained
Untied
Undyed?

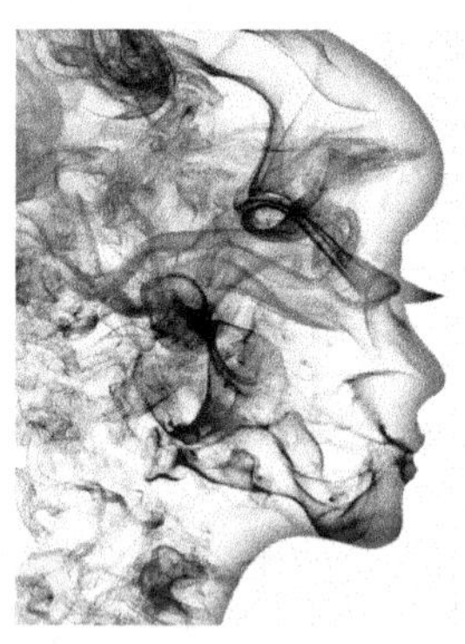

When We Left

There came a time
For the whole to be halves again
How was that possible, though?

How do you divide existence?
How do you separate a life from a lifetime?
Or reduce eternity?

How do you make the ever-expanding
universe small?
How do you let the blood be snatched from
your vein?
Or a picture flee from your brain?

How do you tear off a print immersed into
your skin?
How do you make do without a piece of your
soul?
Or a slice of your heart ripped from the
cracked whole?

It's not just a chunk of me that's gone
I have one of his as well
It's almost a mirror image of mine
We were entwined so

I tried to put it where mine used to be
Needless to say, it doesn't fit
It's all wrong

I wonder which bits of mine left with him
And which remained with me
For I'm sure I didn't leave whole
And neither did he.

A Man From France
(A Limerick)

There once was a man from France
Who never learnt how to dance
He met a dame
Who called his name
And he twirled and spun in a trance.

Oh, Breakfast (An Ode)

Oh, Breakfast, you're tempting
Your menu tantalizing
Choices overwhelming
For a slumberous me

Freshly squeezed orange juice
Cereal and oatmeal
Grits and coffee
Oh, you're waking me!

Toast with butter
Avocado or baked beans
Or peanut butter and jelly
For the foodie in me

Potatoes in their jackets
Or as home fries or hash browns
Bagel with cream cheese
For the vegetarian me

Chai with poha
Pongal or a dosa
Parathas or locha
For the Indian in me

Pita, labneh, olives
Cheung fun or tacos
Teh tarik or ABC
For the traveler in me

Donuts and croissants
Cinnamon roll and scones
Oh, breakfast! You're magic
You royally spoil me!

Nature (A Haiku)

54

Flowers, snow, sunsets
Butterflies and autumn leaves
Colors of nature.

I Am Sorry

I'm sorry
For all the times
I saw you as less
Or as nothing
Or even worse,
Didn't see you at all

I'm sorry
For all the times
I judged you
Like the others did
Without getting
To know you at all

I'm sorry
For how much
I hurt you
From a place of pain
Without thinking
About you at all

I'm sorry
For hearing
The words
Others had spoken
Without listening
To you at all

I'm sorry
It took me
So long
To look in the mirror
And see someone
Who should exist at all

I am sorry
For focusing on
The devastation
And not seeing
Your magic at all.

Dawn And Dusk
(A Haiku)

Skies at dawn and dusk
Purple, pink, red, orange, and
A pinch of yellow.

The gardener's delight

Lily's iris, like
Venus's looking glass
Sweet William's treasure flower

Queen of the meadow,
The sweet sultan,
And morning glory

They rose
To the baby's breath
Violet

The king's spear
The queen's cup
And crown imperial.

The Moon

The moon
When full
Raises tides so high
The waves
Making up
Most of my body
Filling my heart
Welling up in my throat
Threatening to spill
From my eyes
Without so much as a warning
She keeps me awake
Through it all

On some days
When she is calmer
I sneak up on her
She takes me in her arms
And cradles me
Soothing my ebbs
While I tell her
About all that transpired
During that cycle
She listens, patiently
Caressing me
Making me feel at home
In her soft radiance

While on other days,
She teaches me
How to scatter luminescence
Even under another's glorious blaze
While still being present
For the lovers,
The oceans,
The poets,
For those lost in darkness
Or eager to celebrate
To be present
Even in your own fragmented existence
For whomever that looks to you to be whole.

It had to be this way
(A Villanelle)

It is okay that they didn't stay
Your journey had to be till here
It had to be this way

Were they bad to you, or did they stray?
Did they disrespect all that you hold dear?
It is okay that they didn't stay

Maybe they didn't betray, nor leave you
midway
Maybe God removed them for you to be
happier
It had to be this way

Being together made sense yesterday
Though today it hurts that they're nowhere
near
It is okay that they didn't stay

You learnt from each other everyday
But God knew you had to grow further
It had to be this way

Now you'll walk on a new pathway
A higher version of you will appear
It is okay that they didn't stay
It had to be this way.

Goodbye

I find myself on an empty road
Not a single soul around
I walk kicking the pebbles
I stare at the ground

I listen to the silence
The noise bothers my ear
I look up at the day
The darkness hurts around here

The wind howls
The sky cries
I mouth a word
But my voice dies

I try to smile
But it is strained
The strength in me
Seems to have drained

I feel like I am falling
Somewhere deep down below
My consciousness is fading
My instincts are low

I close my eyes; I realize
The sun is finally setting afar
We won't meet, but can surely greet
At a special place under that gleaming star

I'm still that humble earth, you're still the
glorious sky
We'll see the other plenty while we are passing
by
With a tender hug and a final sigh
At the horizon, we'll say goodbye.